THE PIER End

JANE V KING

BALBOA.PRESS

A DIVISION OF HAY HOUSE

Balboa Press books may be ordered through booksellers or by contacting:

Balboa Press
A Division of Hay House
1663 Liberty Drive
Bloomington, IN 47403
www.balboapress.com
844-682-1282

Because of the dynamic nature of the Internet, any web addresses or
links contained in this book may have changed since publication and
may no longer be valid. The views expressed in this work are solely those
of the author and do not necessarily reflect the views of the publisher,
and the publisher hereby disclaims any responsibility for them.

The author of this book does not dispense medical advice or prescribe
the use of any technique as a form of treatment for physical, emotional,
or medical problems without the advice of a physician, either directly
or indirectly. The intent of the author is only to offer information
of a general nature to help you in your quest for emotional and
spiritual well-being. In the event you use any of the information in
this book for yourself, which is your constitutional right, the author
and the publisher assume no responsibility for your actions.

Any people depicted in stock imagery provided by Getty Images are
models, and such images are being used for illustrative purposes only.
Certain stock imagery © Getty Images.

Print information available on the last page.

ISBN: 978-1-9822-5810-8 (sc)
ISBN: 978-1-9822-5811-5 (e)

Library of Congress Control Number: 2020921668

Balboa Press rev. date: 11/02/2020

The Pier End was written in response to a request for a new community play that could celebrate local talent. It has been compared to a medieval mystery play.

The intention is to bring people together in creative celebration to entertain local audiences.

The author finds the end of a pier a mystical place where "earth, sea, and sky all meet." The play was formed by her love of standing alone at the end of a pier, contemplating life.

Any resemblance to real people or places is coincidental.

Contents

Dramatis Personae

Jack, an alternative hero

Narrator

Chloe

Bee

Ella

Counselor Grey

Three "suits"

Eve, Jack's mother

Ensemble of alternative creative people

The Pier End

A Play in Two Acts

Jane King

The Miracle Lyrical Theatre Company

Scene 1

The scene is set at the end of the pier, where sea, earth, and sky meet. There are cloths draped across the pier, with bunting and lights and meaningful symbols suspended everywhere. Headlines from newspapers, Zodiac signs, stars, playing cards are seen. Music of the sea is playing in the background. The other end of the pier, the main entrance, can be seen in the distance.

(Enter Jack. He is beautiful, creative, and dreadlocked.)

JACK. I'm Jack, the alternative mentor here. I create, I advise, I listen intently. Here, where the earth meets the sea and the sky, I care for the people escaping the town, where troubles are greater, oppressive, and looming.

> (*Enter Jack's friends from the pier entrance. They come to him one by one, holding out their hands, and telling him their troubles.*)

FIRST WOMAN. I will be evicted, the landlord has said. I cannot pay such extortionate rent. What can I do? I am working, but art doesn't pay enough.

> (*Jack discretely palms her some money, and she hugs him. She moves to her friend, crying with relief.*)

FIRST MAN. I am not allowed entry into shops in the town. My appearance is otherwise, Asperger's ringing. I need more acceptance and some understanding.

JACK. Here is a list of places of welcome. Tell them Jack sent you, and kindness will come.

> (*The man joins the crowd, looking relieved. Lots of talking, animating people.*)

(*Narrator enters, dressed in white, looking ethereal and wise.*)

NARRATOR. Jack is sage and seer and succor. But if he is the artist, who will paint him? His troubles weigh heavily on him when he's alone. Let's all find a way for our man to be freed.

(*Lively scene where the group play instruments and sing and dance.*)

ENSEMBLE. Pell mell, who can tell
How a community falls into place?
We have a heart that is beating for life.
Unlike the fractured and sad little town,
We have each other; the pier is our realm.
Caring for all with aplomb and hilarity.

JACK. Here my heart is free and singing.
Soaring life surrounds my soul.
A place of beauty where I walk,
Sand and salt of crazy value.

(*The people stroll back to the other end of the pier, singing.*)

JACK. At the other end of the pier, as I see it,
There are heavy problems.
Divisions, diversions, distractions, delusions.
Look closely, and draw your own conclusions.
At the other end of the pier, as we know it,
Are tangles and intrigues and troubles,
relations, restrictions, retractions, reversions.
I reach out and want to find some solutions for the other
end of the pier.

Scene 2

Narrator enters.

NARRATOR. Jack is troubled by his lack of blood family. Solitude brings up his sobbing and pain.

JACK, *crying as he enters.* My father loved the sea, and my mother loved the land. They couldn't work to bridge the gulf; they couldn't understand.
My father sailed away and was never, ever seen again.
And my mother went a-wandering, a-pondering alone.
So effectively, I'm orphaned, even though I'm fully grown.
I miss them ... I need them.
My pier-end behavior is disapproved of and sneered at.

I, Jack, am a faithless man.

For me, three girls who will never understand,

The triplicity, the intrigue, the glorious joy

That I have on the pier, Jack the lad.

I'm not bad; I'm just charming.

They need me ...

Sweet Chloe, Smart Ella, Sad Bee, and me.

Scene 3

The friends gather at the pier end, a wonderful, busy, active rainbow of humanity. It is early morning.

VARIOUS VOICES. The town's in dilemma, the news is out—arson and theft, plastic pollution, unfaithfulness, Brexit woes and confusions, Corona plagues, hatred, divisions and lies, political enmity.
Hear all about it.

(The people go on chanting in the background.)

BEE. Can Jack, my darling, care for me?
I am saddened to my heart.
My parents will not hear me

As I draw my portraits, just existing,
Looked down upon by the wealthy town.
I feel alone and frightened.
I need the strength of Jack,
And I love him to forever.
I will care for him whatever.
I will cherish him and nourish him,
And he will love me back.

Ella. I have money and connections.
My father rules the town.
I don't like him—or my mother—
And I'll bring him down with outrage
With my bit of rough, my Jack.
He's my lover, he's my fun,
And when they know, they'll bellow.

Chloe. I'm not special; I'm just an ordinary girl
Working in a shop,
Selling trinkets to the tourists
And loving Jack with all of me.
My parents are town-damaged
and have withdrawn into their home.
Jack makes my life exciting.
He knows loving and adoring,

Pier-gazing and gold-shoring
In the sand below our feet.

(Enter Jack center stage. The three girls circle him in dance to quiet music. All exit.)

Scene 4

Jack enters alone. The narrator follows.

JACK. Bad Jack. Unfaithful Jack.
I cannot make commitment fully.
Playing around because of hurts
and unfinished business.

NARRATOR. Bring all the strands of his life to his feet,
Here where the shore, clouds, and water all meet.
Heal the heart of our hero, Jack.
Peace is coming back to him.
But patience is needed for tales to unfold.
He has bronze, he has silver, and soon should come gold.

Act 2

Scene 1

Counselor Grey and three suits enter the pier.)

COUNSELOR GREY. This man must be stopped. He subverts, he invents. This Jack is a cannon set loose in the town.
We need order and clarity, by-laws obeyed.
Dress and deportment and all taxes paid.
He must stop the informal, the ragtag, and anarchy.

(Jack enters.)

JACK. Counselor Grey, I come in peace.
You have nothing to fear.
My assembly will welcome you, change you, convince you.

They bring warmth and a willingness, no move to unseat you.
The Pier party moves in mysterious ways, but we achieve.

(*The pier ensemble enter, giving out food and drink to all, sharing care. Narrator enters.*

NARRATOR. Here, where the earth meets the sea and sky,
Soft words led by consideration exchanged,
The hard-set conventions are softened and muted.
Corrections of attitudes, both sides revealing
How moving together contributes to healing.

(*Somehow there is no more gray. Everyone on stage is colorful but not outrageously so.*)

ENSEMBLE. Compromise and compassion have always succeeded in the end. We lift one another.

(*Exit singing.*)

Scene 2

Enter Jack, taking his early morning walk on the pier.

JACK. I have an agony of choice today.
Do I hide or run away?
Bottle it all up deep down inside?
Am I hero-bound or coward-held?
Agony and ecstasy,
Crossroads here in front of me.

(*Ensemble enters.*)

ENSEMBLE. Jack be nimble, Jack Tar,
Jack in the box.
Jack it in, or carry it through.
Jack be quick.

Choose your lady; choose your path.
Be the man.

(*Ensemble exits.*)

Much later, as lights dim, Jack is still on the pier, pacing, restless. A figure walks wearily to the entrance to the pier, collapses, and hides in the shadows. Another figure staggers by, huddled in one of the blankets from the set, and settles in the opposite corner.)

JACK. Trinity of agony, my choices unfold,
The portents are powerful—
Crescent moon, stars, and a cloud of destiny.
I must face it down, be a man.
Not just a leader of motleys
But in charge of myself.

(*Music plays. A baby cries. A mother's voice, "Be still, Jack." A father's voice, "Be great, Jack." Bee walks from the shadows.*)

JACK. Split to the heart, what a glorious sound.

My weakling humanity cracks and responds. I don't know what to do with my life,

Here at the fusion of earth, sea, and sky ...

BEE, *moving to Jack.* You have cared for me, Jack, in my sadness and art.

You have loved me to forever, and I have loved you back.

We have made a little baby, deep inside.

It has been my secret, for Ella and Chloe seem to overshadow me.

JACK, *embracing her, touching the bump, overcome.* My little Bee, my lover, and a child of our own coming to our world.

I crack, I fall, I falter, but your love will make me strong.

Here is a miracle

(*The larger bundle shifts, coughing. Eve emerges, very disheveled.*)

EVE. I'm not what you think; I have traveled but stayed in good places.

I am seeking my son, but my money ran out yesterday.

The pier has woken me; I heard voices.

JACK, *astonished*. Mother, Eve, it's you at last.

My last letter must have reached you. (*Jack and Eve embrace.*)

EVE. I was on the other coast, still hoping Dan would return from the sea. We could then search for our Jack together.

Who is your lady, carrying a baby?

BEE. This is the child our true love has brought.

I know that Jack loves us to the ends of the earth.

I tested him and saw in his eyes he is true.

This has brought him to me and now brought us to you. (*The family embraces, and there are many tears.*)

(*Narrator enters.*)

NARRATOR. If you have patience, it will be rewarded. The cosmic genetics have power and persistence.

Jack will now settle down

Here in this strange old town.

Respect for him growing, the strange pier-end sage,

He has earned his redemption on this salty stage.

(*Blackout*)

Scene 3

Ensemble enters at the other end of the pier. They are painting, sewing, making music, dancing, juggling, and so on. New blankets, bright with color and hopeful symbols, are hung up. The sun is shining.)

JACK. Here, where the earth meets the sea and the sky,
A banquet of joy is laid out for today.
I am contented; yes, Jack is contented
Here with the family trinity gathered,
All for one, and one for all.

COUNSELOR GREY. Jack, come and join us and help with the town.
It needs your mind, all your joy, all your soul.
Reach through the gate and bring us solutions,

Jack the enhancer, the lover, the man. (*He embraces Ella, his daughter.*)

CHLOE. My parents have come into sunshine today.
Their fear of the town has been moved by events.
I am freed by the joy, and tomorrow I'll thrive,
borne on excitement, just being alive.
My parents have courage, no longer are cowed.
They are safe, they are happy in this wondrous crowd. (*She embraces her parents.*)

ELLA. I am humbled, no longer a princess of style.
I can see very clearly, and well up with joy.
I can move on, help make kindness a habit.
The town will arise in a fervor of care.
I will respect, I will lift, I will dance with the town.
No longer a few up, the others pushed down.

NARRATOR. Signs and symbols, lights and loves
Move forward now, together.
Babies can't have too much love.
The guardians gather at this pier,
Brought here together by earth, sea, sky,
and people's hearts beating.
Little one, a towering force,
Tilting heads to mirror life,

Warming those who will witness her coming.

EVE. Jack, my boy, ahoy!
A ship sails from the pier
Taking negatives away.
Let's celebrate the ebbs and flows of life today.

JACK. Stitch the patchwork, weave the web,
Sewn together, now, forever.
Ties to bind us, generations,
Closeness, other new sensations.
The family is coming home
At the other end of the pier!

(*There is joy and celebration. A pier party
begins.*)

NARRATOR. Where is your earth and your sky
and sea?
Bring them together, and see how they frame
Your needs and your wants and your thoughts.
In this voyage, try making the most of your lives.
Go well, and muse on the joy of Jack's glory.
And make your own happiness shine in your story.

The Pier-End Songs

To be set to music and used as appropriate
in various places in the play.

Earth, Sea, Sky Song
Horizon
Weaving
Triangle of Nature
The Song of Jack

Earth, Sea, Sky Song

The woman of the earth,
Who grounds the man possessed,
Is filled with hope and love.
She gives her heart.
She makes the living world
With artistry and grace.
She forms the future scene.
She gives.
A bee is of the land
And grounded in her hive,
Securing, easing pain.
She gives her heart.

The modern woman swims
With salt and strength and power.
Ambition is her drive.
She takes her toll.
She ebbs and flows with pace.
She sweeps aside the sand.
She cleans unwanted dross.
She takes
The sailors on their shore.

Respect her awesome drive.
She stops the drift in life.
She takes her toll.

A spirit of the sky
Can hide and yet exist.
A subtle force, not clear.
She shares her soul.
She wraps her world in mist,
A gentle, peaceful cloud,
Not sure of where she goes.
She shares.
Her nuance takes you up
Above the daily world,
Gives sight to clouded eyes.
She shares her soul.

Horizon

In one turn you can see the whole horizon.
New aspects fill your eyes and move your mind.
Looking out the other way,
What is it you see today?
Which human story are you going to find?

At the other end of the pier
There are differences.
At the other end of the pier
Sadness and pain.
The other world we witness
Is beyond those gates,
With people who need help
For loss or gain.

At the other end of the pier
There are challenges.
At the other end of the pier
Torment and fear.
This other world we witness
Needs some happiness,
With people who want help
At the other end of the pier.

Weaving

The thread of inheritance stitches again.
A child of two houses united in one.
Each feature created by natural dancing,
The mysterious process of life and its dicing.

The future direction must first recognize
The inborn, the settled collection of skills.
Each move will depend on the program inherent,
The mystical weaving that humans inherit.

Triangle of Nature

Our deepest cries are carried in the air.
The salt sea washes out the pain and fear.
The ground is steady underneath our feet,
Where ocean, cloud, and sand conspire to meet.
And Gaia's healing touches our despair.

Our newborn self has freedom from all care.
The family will love with all its hearts.
The natural response is clear and sweet,
Where earth and sky and sea conspire to meet,
And all our lives are gathered here to share.

The Song of Jack

It's that end of the pier that needs changing.
That end has its troubles, you know.
Squabbles and strife,
Disruption of life,
Malcontentment.

Let's all look at the sad situations.
Let's work on a plan to produce
A harmonious plan.
Every woman and man
Great enjoyment.

We have started to bind the stitches.
We hope for a future of calm,
Peacefulness rife,
Healing of life,
Just enchantment.

Printed in the United States
By Bookmasters